Define Yourself

A 40 Day Journey of Empowerment

By
DeGeorge Griffin

First Edition

Paperback ISBN 978-1-971868-27-1

Cover Design & Layout by M.G. Morris

Dedication

To the memory of my beloved Nana
whose wisdom, love, and guidance built the
foundation that my family stands on.

Table of Contents

TABLE OF CONTENTS

Introduction

Labels and identities are used to claim or bestow power, which is defined as the ability to produce an effect and the possession of control. Whether we recognize it or not, life constantly presents us with moments when power is being negotiated. Power and control flow externally through spheres of influence, institutions, and expectations, but more importantly, internally through the beliefs we hold about ourselves.

In many ways, life is a continuous struggle for power. Not necessarily power over others, but power over our own thoughts, decisions, direction, and identity. I wanted to begin this journey by exploring the concept of power, because once we understand how power operates in our lives, we begin to understand the importance of claiming authority over our own paths.

When we realize that our lives are profoundly impacted by our ability to self-actualize, we begin to understand how important it is to take ownership of who we are becoming.

This journey is designed to help you recognize that power already exists within you.

The goal of this book is simple but profound, to provide guidance and tools that help you embrace your inner strength, clarify your mindset, and take ownership of the narrative of your life. This is not a book about perfection. It is a book about progress.

I would like to invite you to commit to a forty day journey with me.

Why forty days?

Throughout history and across cultures, the number forty has symbolized transformation, preparation, and renewal. It represents a period of reflection, challenge and, ultimately, emergence into something new. Forty days signifies a cycle of growth that leads to clarity and completion.

In this journey, I invite you to dedicate just five minutes each day to reflect with intentional thought. These daily moments are designed to help center you, quiet the noise around you, and reconnect you with your purpose. Small, consistent moments of reflection can produce powerful changes over time. Just as a river slowly shapes the landscape around it, intentional thought shapes the direction of our lives.

Over the next forty days, we will explore powerful ideas and practical perspectives designed to strengthen your inner foundation. The themes we will unpack together focus on identity and purpose, alignment, resilience and adversity, focus and execution, confidence and mindset, self-care, the power of community, change management, leadership, and life perspective.

Each theme represents a pillar that supports a meaningful and balanced life. These concepts are not abstract theories. They are lessons drawn from lived experiences, challenges, observations, and moments of reflection that have helped shape my own journey.

One of the inspirations that led me to create this forty day journey came during a period of major life transitions. Life has a way of presenting inflection points, moments where we are forced to pause, reflect, and reconsider who we are becoming. During times like these, wisdom becomes invaluable.

In my own life, one of the wisest individuals I have ever known was my nana/grandmother. She had a perspective on life that was both practical and hopeful. I use the word practical intentionally because meaningful progress must always be grounded in reality. Dreams without action remain dreams. Movement must be anchored in discipline and effort.

At the same time, she embodied a powerful sense of hope. Hope is not naive optimism. Hope is the belief that even when circumstances appear difficult, there is still a path forward. Hope carries with it the faith that perseverance, patience, and integrity will ultimately lead to something greater.

It is through the combination of clear thinking, discipline, and hope that we learn to move forward. My nana's outlook taught me that resilience and optimism are not opposites of realism, but instead, they are complements to it.

Before we begin this journey together, I want you to understand:

There is no label, identity, description, or category that can define who you are.

Society often attempts to categorize individuals based on a variety of factors, heritage, skin color, ethnicity, economic background, geography, education, profession, and countless other identifiers. While these characteristics may describe aspects of our lives, they do not determine our potential.

You are far more than any label that
society attempts to place upon you.

At any point in time, you have the ability to decide who you are and who you are becoming. Identity is not something that should be imposed upon you. Identity is something that must be claimed by you.

In ancient times, leaders often emerged by expressing interest, gaining influence, and taking responsibility within their communities. Over time, many societies shifted from leadership based on merit and influence to leadership determined by bloodlines. Kingdoms and nations began to pass power through hereditary systems, and this is where the concept of royalty derived, which is where power being passed down from generation to generation began to take hold.

But there is a deeper truth hidden within that history.

Each of us carries a form of royalty within our own lives. Not in the sense of ruling over others, but in the sense of possessing authority over our own destiny.

You are the ruler of your decisions.

You are the steward of your potential.

You are the author of your life's story.

When we allow society, circumstances, or the opinions of others to dictate who we are, we surrender the authority that already belongs to us. The truth is simple; each of us is the king or queen of our own life.

Real power does not begin with status, money, or influence. Power begins in the mind.

The thoughts we choose to believe about ourselves shape the decisions we make. Those decisions shape our habits. Those habits shape our outcomes. Confidence, clarity, and belief are the starting points of transformation.

There is a saying that captures this idea perfectly. *You change your life when you change your mind.*

When your mindset changes, your perspective changes. When your perspective changes, your actions change. And when your actions change consistently over time, your life changes.

So here is my challenge to you:

1. Commit to your personal growth.
2. Commit to the belief that change is possible.
3. Commit to recognizing the power that already exists within you.

Over the next forty days, I encourage you to approach each reflection with openness and honesty. Some days will inspire you. Other days may challenge you. Some days may cause you to reflect deeply on areas of your life that require attention.

That is part of the process.

Growth requires both courage and humility.

But if you remain committed to the journey, you will discover something powerful. You are far more capable than you ever imagined, far stronger than you give yourself credit for, and far closer to your purpose than you may currently realize.

You already possess the power to define yourself.

So take a deep breath.

Turn the page and let's get started; the journey toward defining yourself begins now.

Identity and Purpose

Day 1

The most powerful act in the world is the ability to Define Yourself.

DAILY INSIGHT

The only person who can tell you who you are is you! To define yourself, is to reject the passive role of being shaped by circumstances, and instead, step into the role of the mastermind of your own identity. It means recognizing that your story, your purpose, and your direction are not predetermined by your environment but are determined by your conscious choices.

This ability requires courage, discipline, and clarity. Growth begins the moment you stop allowing external voices to dictate who you are and decide who you will become. Every meaningful moment in life, whether personal, professional, or spiritual, starts with an establishment of identity. When you define yourself, you reclaim authority over your mindset, your standards and, most importantly, your future. You stop reacting to life and begin directing it. Today starts the first day of your new outlook on life when you will shift into a purpose led identity.

MOMENT OF REFLECTION

How have you allowed people, circumstances, or your past experiences to define who you are? What would change if you reclaimed the power to define yourself instead?

INTENTIONAL APPLICATION

Write a personal definition statement and in one or two sentences, clearly define the person you are today and who you desire to be moving forward. Remember this is your opportunity to control your own narrative and this should be based in line with both your purpose and life goals.

PERSONAL INSIGHTS

Day 2

The moment you decide to thrive instead of survive, life begins to meet you at the point of your expectation.

DAILY INSIGHT

There is a major difference between surviving and thriving. Survival is reactive and it is that mindset that keeps you focused solely on how to get through any given day, responding to circumstances as they come and accepting whatever life hands you. Thriving is focused on flourishing and walking in prosperity. Thriving starts with a decision to rise above limitation and to approach life with expectation, purpose, and belief in what is possible. The moment you make that internal shift, your perspective changes, your actions change, and eventually, your outcomes begin to change as well.

Life has a remarkable way of responding to the level of expectation we carry. When we expect little, we often settle for little. However, when we have high expectations, opportunity and greatness begin to align on our behalf. Thriving produces thoughts, habits, and discipline that align with our expectations. Thriving is not something that happens by accident, but it is the result of choosing to believe that more is possible and that we are worthy of our dreams.

MOMENT OF REFLECTION

Where in your life have you been operating in survival mode, and what can you change today to shift that area of your life to a mindset of thriving instead?

INTENTIONAL APPLICATION

Choose one area of your life, whether it be your health, work, relationships, or your own personal growth, where you feel you have an opportunity to level up. Write down one higher expectation you have for that area and identify one action you can take today to move toward a thriving mindset rather than a survival mindset.

PERSONAL INSIGHTS

Day 3

Imperfections are part of the process for developing you into your purpose.

DAILY INSIGHT

Give yourself grace and be patient with your process of living a purposeful life. The human condition focuses on trying to avoid mistakes, hide our flaws, or only present a polished version of our personality to the world. Yet the truth is that growth has never been born from perfection. Imperfections, including our setbacks, missteps, doubts, and failures, often are the very experiences that provide revelation and insights that shape our character. Imperfections refine our perspective, deepen our humility, and teach us lessons for balanced living.

Purpose is not discovered in a moment of perfection; however, it is revealed through the process of becoming. Each challenge, each failure, and each growth area is part of a larger development process that propels us to completing the calling on our life. When we stop viewing our imperfections as weaknesses and begin to see them as tools for growth, we unlock a deeper level of self-acceptance and resilience. In this way, the very things we once thought disqualified us often become the foundation of our purpose.

MOMENT OF REFLECTION

How are you dealing with the imperfections and growth areas of your life?

INTENTIONAL APPLICATION

Write down one lesson you have learned from dealing with imperfections and reflect on how you can apply that learning experience to your personal development.

PERSONAL INSIGHTS

DAY 4

Greatness is directly connected to consistency. Once a plan is in place, anything outside of your plan is a distraction.

DAILY INSIGHT

Greatness is rarely the result of a single, extraordinary moment. Instead, it is the product of consistent actions repeated over time with clarity and discipline. When you commit to a meaningful plan, whether it is related to your purpose, career, health, or personal development, create a roadmap that guides your decisions. The power of that plan is not just in what is written down, but in the daily commitment to follow it with focus and intention.

Distractions are one of the greatest threats to progress. Life is always going to life, and unexpected demands constantly compete for your attention. While some may appear valuable in the moment, anything that pulls you away from the direction you have intentionally chosen will likely slow your progress. Consistency requires discipline and the ability to remain committed to your plan even when distractions arise. When you stay focused on the path you have set, your consistent effort compounds over time, turning small, daily actions into meaningful results.

MOMENT OF REFLECTION

What is one defined plan or goal that you have for your life, and what specific distractions have been preventing you from consistently executing your plan?

INTENTIONAL APPLICATION

Greatness is built through consistent execution of a clear plan. Write down one goal and develop a plan to help you achieve your goal. Then identify one distraction that regularly pulls you away from executing. How can you commit to being more deliberate to eliminate or limit that distraction and take one focused action that moves your plan forward?

PERSONAL INSIGHTS

Day 5

Growth is learning to accept the unknown with unshakable faith that things will work out. A fresh start begins in your mind and the belief that when you change your outlook, you change your life.

DAILY INSIGHT

Learning to trust that life will work is a difficult concept; growth occurs when we accept that boundaries of certainty almost never exist. Most meaningful transformation begins the moment we step into the unknown and when we move forward without having every answer. Scriptures tell us that faith is the substance of things hoped for and the evidence of things not seen, so we must realize that our effort, resilience, and purpose will guide us. We must realize that accepting the unknown is not about ignoring fear; it is about refusing to allow fear to control your decisions. It requires the belief that even when the path is unclear, progress is still possible.

A fresh start does not always come from changing your environment or circumstances; it begins with changing the way you see them. Your mindset shapes the way you interpret challenges, opportunities, and setbacks. When you shift your outlook from doubt to possibility, and from hesitation to belief, you begin to open doors that once seemed closed. Growth is less about waiting for the perfect moment and more about choosing to see possibility where uncertainty once lived.

MOMENT OF REFLECTION

What area of your life currently feels uncertain or unknown, and how might your life change if you approached that uncertainty with faith instead of fear?

INTENTIONAL APPLICATION

Growth begins the moment you move forward with faith, even when the full path is not yet visible. Identify one situation in your life where uncertainty has been holding you back from taking action. Write down one small step that will help you move forward; the goal is to simply get started.

PERSONAL INSIGHTS

Alignment and The Importance of Self-Care

Day 6

True investment in yourself means sharpening your talents, pursuing what brings you joy, and trusting that the sacrifices you make today are the price of your future success.

DAILY INSIGHT

The most valuable investment you will ever make cannot be found in stock markets, businesses, or possessions, but it is in yourself. Investing in yourself means taking the time to refine your abilities, strengthen your discipline, and develop the talents that make you unique. It requires intentional effort to grow in areas that align with your purpose and to nurture the passions that bring meaning and fulfillment to your life. When you commit to developing your talents and doing the intentional work that brings you genuine joy, you begin to build a foundation for a life of purpose and impact.

Success in life also requires sacrifice. The path to growth often asks you to give up what is easy, comfortable, or immediately gratifying. Whether it is sacrificing time, convenience, or temporary pleasure, these decisions create space for long-term success. Every moment spent improving yourself is a deposit into your future. When you trust that today's discipline and sacrifice will lead to tomorrow's rewards, you begin to see that investing in yourself is not a loss; it is the most powerful commitment you can make to your future.

MOMENT OF REFLECTION

What talent, skill, or passion in your life needs greater investment of energy from you, and what short-term sacrifices might you need to make to fully develop it?

INTENTIONAL APPLICATION

Choose one talent or skill that you believe is important for your future. Write down one thing that you can do today, intentionally, to develop it. View this time as a deposit into your future success, reminding yourself that every intentional investment in your growth compounds over time.

PERSONAL INSIGHTS

Day 7

Your personal well-being and healing are your first priority; restoration is a critical component to a balanced life.

DAILY INSIGHT

In a world that constantly pushes us to perform, produce, and achieve, it can be easy to neglect the most important foundation to our success, which is our well-being. True growth and purpose cannot flourish when we are exhausted, emotionally drained, or disconnected from ourselves. Personal healing and restoration are not signs of weakness or delay; they are essential investments in the sustainability of our lives. When we prioritize our mental, emotional, and physical health, we create the stability necessary to pursue our goals with clarity and strength.

Restoration is a powerful but often overlooked component of balance. Just as our bodies need rest after physical exertion, our mind needs stillness after intense focus. Our lives require intentional moments of regeneration. Taking time to restore yourself allows you to regain perspective, strengthen your resilience, and reconnect with what truly matters. A balanced life is not one without challenges; however, it is one where restoration is intentionally woven into the rhythm of living.

MOMENT OF REFLECTION

In what areas of your life have you been prioritizing productivity or responsibility at the expense of your personal well-being and healing?

INTENTIONAL APPLICATION

Set aside a dedicated period of time today for intentional restoration. Use this time to engage in something that renews your energy and supports your well-being, such as taking a quiet walk, journaling, meditating, or simply disconnecting from external demands. Write down what you will do today to care for your well-being.

PERSONAL INSIGHTS

Day 8

Discernment is a super power and it must be used daily.

DAILY INSIGHT

Discernment is the ability to see clearly and to distinguish what is helpful from what is harmful. It also causes us to determine what is meaningful from what is merely noise and what aligns with your purpose from what distracts you from it. In a world filled with constant opinions, opportunities, and influences competing for your attention, discernment becomes the most valuable ability that you can develop. It allows you to feel, evaluate, and choose your actions wisely rather than reacting impulsively to every situation that presents itself.

Like any true strength, discernment must be practiced consistently. Every day presents decisions about where to invest your time, who to trust, what opportunities to pursue, and which distractions to ignore. When you cultivate discernment, you begin to move through life with greater clarity and confidence. Instead of being pulled in many directions, you learn to align your decisions with your values, your goals, and your purpose. Over time, this discipline of thoughtful decision-making becomes a powerful force that protects your growth and strengthens the direction of your life.

MOMENT OF REFLECTION

Where in your life right now do you need to exercise greater discernment? This could be in your choices, relationships, opportunities, or the way you spend your time.

INTENTIONAL APPLICATION

Get in the habit of asking yourself three questions:

1. Does this align with my values and long term goals?
2. Will this move me closer to the person I want to become?
3. Is this an opportunity or a distraction?

Write down how you plan to strengthen your discernment and ensure that your daily choices reflect the life you are intentionally building.

PERSONAL INSIGHTS

Day 9

Embracing the act of being vulnerable is not weakness, as it allows you to tap into authenticity. Give yourself permission to hit the pause button and take a personal timeout to refocus on the things that matter.

DAILY INSIGHT

Vulnerability can feel uncomfortable or even risky; however, vulnerability is not a sign of weakness as it is the doorway to authenticity. When you allow yourself to be honest about your emotions, challenges, and uncertainties, you begin to live from a place of truth rather than performance. Authenticity grows when we stop trying to appear flawless and, instead, embrace the fullness of who we are.

The most difficult step forward is not pushing harder, but it is intentionally pausing. Life moves quickly, and it is easy to become consumed by responsibilities, expectations, and external pressures. Giving yourself permission to pause allows you to reconnect with your priorities, regain clarity, and realign with what truly matters. These moments of stillness create space for honesty, self-awareness, and renewed purpose. Vulnerability and reflection work together, and when they are practiced properly, they become powerful tools that guide you toward a more balanced and authentic life.

MOMENT OF REFLECTION

When was the last time you allowed yourself to pause long enough to be honest about what you are truly feeling and what truly matters in your life?

INTENTIONAL APPLICATION

Schedule time to take a personal pause for at least ten minutes, with no distractions. Use this time to quietly reflect on what currently matters the most in your life right now and whether your daily routine aligns with those priorities. During this moment, practice being honest with yourself about where you may need to slow down, ask for support, or realign your focus. Authenticity begins when you give yourself permission to pause, reflect, and lead your life with truth. Write down how to demonstrate authenticity.

PERSONAL INSIGHTS

Day 10

Strategic redirection is one of God's greatest forms of protection, and it produces divine alignment.

DAILY INSIGHT

Life does not always go according to plan, and at times, it can move in a direction we did not expect. Plans change, opportunities close, and paths we once believed were meant for us cease. In those moments, it is easy to interpret redirection as failure, rejection, or loss. However, what feels like disruption is actually protection. Strategic redirection can be a powerful reminder that not every door is meant for you. Some doors close to guide you to something greater and towards what aligns more fully with your purpose.

Divine alignment often occurs through experiences we did not anticipate. When we trust that certain shifts in our lives are not accidents but part of a greater design, we begin to see challenges differently. Instead of resisting change, we learn to look for the wisdom and direction within it. Growth requires the belief that even when the path ahead seems uncertain, every redirection is shaping us, positioning us, and preparing us for what is truly meant for us.

MOMENT OF REFLECTION

Can you identify a moment in your life when what initially felt like a setback or rejection eventually revealed itself to be a form of protection or redirection?

INTENTIONAL APPLICATION

Take a moment today to reflect on one area of your life where things have not unfolded according to your original plan. Instead of viewing it as a setback, write down three possible ways this redirection might be guiding you:

1. Toward a better opportunity
2. Teaching you a life lesson
3. Aligning with your purpose

By reframing redirection as protection, you begin to trust the process and remain open to the path that is unfolding before you.

PERSONAL INSIGHTS

Resilience and Adversity

Day 11

Challenges present the opportunity for revelation to occur, and embracing new perspectives allows us to triumph over what was meant to destroy our peace. Time is the true revealer if someone is a supporter or a detractor.

DAILY INSIGHT

Challenges often can feel overwhelming and unfair. Yet within every challenge, lies an opportunity. Difficult circumstances produce truths that might otherwise remain hidden. In difficult moments, you realize your own strength. When we face adversity with openness and reflection, we gain new perspectives that allow us to grow rather than become consumed by the difficulty itself.

The fullness of time reveals the true nature of both situations and relationships. People who genuinely support your growth will often become clearer during moments of struggle, while those who drain your energy or disrupt your peace may also reveal themselves. Embracing new perspectives allows you to see these revelations, not as discouragement, but as guidance. Challenges produce opportunities to protect your peace, strengthen your resilience, and align your life with those who truly support your journey.

MOMENT OF REFLECTION

Think about a recent challenge in your life. What truths about yourself or the people around you has that experience begun to reveal?

INTENTIONAL APPLICATION

Reflect on one current challenge or difficult situation in your life. Write down one lesson or new perspective that this challenge may be revealing to you. Then consider whether there is a person in your life whose actions during this time have demonstrated genuine support or revealed the opposite. Use this clarity to make one intentional decision today that protects your peace and aligns you with people and choices that support your growth.

PERSONAL INSIGHTS

Day 12

Seasons change and we must learn to put ourselves first and accept others as they are; acceptance is admitting that even when we do our best to make a situation work and it does not, then we must move away from misalignment.

DAILY INSIGHT

Life unfolds through seasons of time, and each season brings new experiences, relationships, and lessons. Just as nature transitions from one phase to another, our lives also evolve. Sometimes we hold on to situations, environments, or relationships long after they have served their purpose because we believe that with enough effort, we can make them work. While perseverance is valuable, wisdom also requires the ability to recognize when something is no longer aligned with our growth, values, or peace.

Acceptance is not giving up; it is acknowledging reality with clarity and maturity. It means understanding that despite our best intentions and efforts, not every situation is meant to continue in the same form. Accepting others as they are allows us to release unrealistic expectations and focus on what we can control, which are our own choices, boundaries, and direction. When we recognize misalignment and have the courage to step away from it, we create space for new opportunities, healthier connections, and personal growth that better aligns with the life we are meant to live.

MOMENT OF REFLECTION

Is there a situation or relationship in your life where you have been trying to force alignment, even though deep down you sense that the season may be changing?

INTENTIONAL APPLICATION

Take a few moments today to reflect on one area of your life where you may feel tension or misalignment. Write down what you have been trying to make work and honestly assess whether it still aligns with your well-being and your long term growth. Identify one boundary, adjustment, or step you can take today that honors your peace and allows you to move toward greater alignment in the next season of your life.

PERSONAL INSIGHTS

Day 13

The only way to lose in life is to give up; trust that your journey is not a mistake. No matter the circumstance, I will compartmentalize and conquer.

DAILY INSIGHT

Life rarely unfolds exactly as we imagine. Along the journey, we encounter setbacks, unexpected turns, and moments that challenge our confidence and resolve. In those moments, it can be tempting to believe that the obstacles we face are signs that we have taken the wrong path. Yet the truth is that every experience, including both the victories and the struggles play a role in shaping who we become. The only true loss in life occurs when we allow doubt or discouragement to convince us to stop moving forward.

Compartmentalizing challenges is a powerful discipline that allows us to navigate difficult circumstances without becoming overwhelmed by them. Instead of allowing every problem to consume our entire mindset, we learn to address each challenge with focus and perspective. By breaking obstacles into manageable pieces and maintaining faith in the process, we develop resilience and clarity. When you trust that your journey has purpose and refuse to surrender to adversity, you cultivate the mindset needed to overcome obstacles and continue progressing toward your goals.

MOMENT OF REFLECTION

Are there any challenges in your life that have made you question your path? How could changing your perspective on a challenge shift your mindset?

INTENTIONAL APPLICATION

Identify one challenge that has been weighing on your mind. Instead of viewing it as one overwhelming problem, break it into three smaller actions or steps you can take to begin addressing it. Focus on completing just one step today and write down that first step. By compartmentalizing the challenge and taking deliberate action, you remind yourself that progress is possible and that perseverance, not perfection, is the key to conquering life's obstacles.

PERSONAL INSIGHTS

Day 14

Resilience in the face of adversity produces character, and struggle produces success. Never forget to seize the opportunity that emerges from enduring hardships.

DAILY INSIGHT

Adversity is often viewed as something to avoid, yet some of life's most important lessons are born through difficulty. When we encounter hardship, we are given an opportunity to develop resilience, which is the ability to endure challenges without losing our sense of determination. Each obstacle tests our patience, our courage, and our belief in what is possible. Over time, these experiences strengthen our character and shape the person we become. What once felt like a burden can ultimately become the training ground that prepares us for greater responsibility and achievement.

Struggle is also one of the greatest teachers of success. The challenges we face force us to adapt, think creatively, and push beyond what we thought were limits. Hidden within many hardships are opportunities for growth, wisdom, and unexpected breakthroughs. Those who learn to persevere through difficulty often discover that the very experiences they once feared were the same experiences that prepared them for future success. By choosing resilience and remaining open to the lessons within struggle, we transform adversity into a powerful catalyst for progress.

MOMENT OF REFLECTION

Can you identify a hardship in your life that, although difficult at the time, ultimately strengthened your character or prepared you for a greater opportunity?

INTENTIONAL APPLICATION

Take a moment to identify one strength that a current or past struggle has developed within you. This can be patience, resilience, courage, or discipline. Write down and acknowledge how that strength has helped shape the person you are becoming.

PERSONAL INSIGHTS

Day 15

Clear blue skies are above even the worst clouds.

DAILY INSIGHT

One of the most exciting things about flying is when you reach beyond the clouds and you enter into an atmosphere that feels serene. Life inevitably brings moments that feel heavy and overwhelming which can obscure our sense of hope. In those moments, it can be difficult to remember that circumstances, like clouds in the sky, are temporary. Just as the darkest storm cannot permanently erase the blue sky above it, difficult seasons in life do not define the entirety of our journey. Instead, we must remember that difficulty will inevitably pass and that it comes to test our patience, strengthen our resilience, and remind us of the importance of perseverance.

Growth often requires the discipline to maintain perspective during difficult times. When we remember that clearer days exist beyond the clouds of our current struggles, we cultivate hope and resilience. This perspective allows us to endure hardship without losing sight of possibility. Even when circumstances appear uncertain, the promise of clear skies reminds us that challenges are part of the journey, and that they are not the final destination. Holding on to that belief gives us the strength to continue moving forward.

MOMENT OF REFLECTION

What helps you remember that your current setbacks or circumstances are temporary and that clearer days are still ahead?

INTENTIONAL APPLICATION

Identify one growth area or concern that has been weighing on your mind. Now, write down one positive outcome or opportunity that could eventually emerge from navigating this experience.

Reminding yourself that the "clear sky" still exists above the clouds can help you approach challenges with patience, perspective, and renewed hope.

PERSONAL INSIGHTS

Focus and Execution

Day 16

The best way to grow is to be accountable and focus on making progress one day at a time.

DAILY INSIGHT

Daily progress can produce dramatic transformation. When we take consistent actions day after day, it pushes us to results. Accountability plays a critical role in the process because it requires us to take ownership of our choices, our habits, and our progress. When we hold ourselves accountable, we move beyond excuses and begin to intentionally shape the direction of our lives. This mindset encourages honesty with ourselves about where we are and what steps we must take in the future.

Focusing on progress one day at a time helps prevent us from becoming overwhelmed by the larger journey ahead. Long term goals can sometimes feel distant or intimidating, but when we concentrate on what can be improved today, then growth becomes manageable and sustainable. Discipline grows through these daily commitments, and over time, those small steps accumulate into meaningful change. By embracing accountability and valuing daily progress, we create a rhythm of growth that steadily moves us toward the life we are striving to build.

MOMENT OF REFLECTION

In what area of your life could greater personal accountability help you make steady progress toward the person you want to become?

INTENTIONAL APPLICATION

Choose one personal growth goal that matters to you. Write down one specific action you can take today that moves you closer to that goal, no matter how small. Challenge yourself to complete that action before the end of today, reminding yourself that consistent daily progress is the foundation of transformational growth.

PERSONAL INSIGHTS

Day 17

When you are in flow, the miraculous becomes possible; there is power in being intentional.

DAILY INSIGHT

There are moments in life when everything seems to align, which causes your focus to sharpen, your energy to be productive, and your actions to feel purposeful. This is often described as being "in flow"—a state where clarity and momentum work together to move you forward. Flow does not happen by accident; it is often the result of intentional choices. When you are clear about your priorities and disciplined in your actions, you create the conditions for progress and possibility to emerge. In this state, obstacles feel less overwhelming and solutions become more visible.

Intentionality is the catalyst that brings flow into your life. Living intentionally means making sound decisions about how you spend your time, where you invest your energy, and what direction you want your life to move toward. When your actions align with your purpose and your focus is guided by intention, you create space for extraordinary outcomes. What may once have seemed impossible begins to feel attainable because you are moving with clarity and resolve.

MOMENT OF REFLECTION

How could greater intentionality help you move away from feelings of uncertainty to heightened focus which produces flow?

INTENTIONAL APPLICATION

Choose one high priority from your to-do list and write down the single most meaningful action that will move that priority forward. Commit to completing that action with full focus and without distraction.

By directing your attention and energy with intention, you begin to create the conditions where momentum builds and meaningful progress is made.

PERSONAL INSIGHTS

Day 18

Procrastination prolongs struggle and postpones gratification, when we improve our focus, we conquer delay.

DAILY INSIGHT

Procrastination is the true enemy of progress and it often disguises itself as temporary relief. When we delay a task, decision, or responsibility, it may feel like a brief sense of calm in the moment. Yet that comfort is usually short-lived, because the unfinished task continues to occupy our thoughts and it can drain our energy. Over time, procrastination creates a cycle that can cause anxiety and dysfunction because the time that once was abundant is now fleeting. What could have been resolved with focused action becomes a growing source of stress and distraction.

The antidote to procrastination is intentional focus. When we direct our attention toward what truly needs to be done, we reclaim control over our time and our goals. Discipline is not about eliminating difficulty; it is about choosing progress despite it. By strengthening our ability to focus and act with purpose, we reduce the mental weight of unfinished tasks and create momentum in our lives. Each small step taken with focus moves us closer to achieving our goals.

MOMENT OF REFLECTION

What task, goal, or decision have you been postponing that could push you toward progress and peace of mind if you chose to address it today?

INTENTIONAL APPLICATION

Select one task or responsibility that you have been putting off and commit to working on it today. Remove distractions during that time and give your full attention to starting the task. Write down which task you will accomplish.

Often the hardest part of overcoming procrastination is beginning. Once you take the first step with focused intention, momentum naturally begins to follow.

PERSONAL INSIGHTS

Day 19

Asking for help is another form of self-love; you do not have to do everything yourself.

DAILY INSIGHT

It is time to challenge the belief that strength means handling everything alone. We often feel pressure to solve every problem, manage every responsibility, and overcome every obstacle without assistance. While independence can be valuable, true strength also includes the wisdom to recognize when support is needed. Asking for help is not a sign of weakness; it is an act of self-awareness and self-respect. It reflects the understanding that growth is often accelerated when we allow others to share their expertise, experience, and encouragement.

Self-love involves caring for your well-being and recognizing your limits without judgment. When you ask for help, you acknowledge that you deserve support and that you do not have to carry every burden by yourself. Life is built on relationships, collaboration, and shared understanding. By opening yourself to guidance and assistance, you create opportunities for deeper connection and personal growth. In doing so, you remind yourself that progress does not always require doing everything alone; instead, it requires the courage to invite people whom you trust into your journey.

MOMENT OF REFLECTION

Is there an area of your life where you have been carrying the weight alone, even though support or guidance might help you move forward more effectively?

INTENTIONAL APPLICATION

What is one challenge, task, or goal where support could make a difference? Reach out to one person you trust, a mentor, friend, colleague, or family member, and ask for their perspective, advice, or assistance. Write down whom you will reach out to and set a completion timeline; remember, it is easier to get help when you are specific with your needs. By allowing yourself to receive support, you are practicing self-love.

PERSONAL INSIGHTS

Day 20

Success sometimes takes longer because you are strategically executing your vision; patient progress is the key.

DAILY INSIGHT

In a world that often celebrates instant results and overnight success, it can be easy to feel discouraged when progress takes longer than you expected. Remember that meaningful success is rarely built quickly. When you are intentionally and strategically working toward a vision, progress may unfold gradually as you refine your skills, learn from experience, and strengthen your foundation. Patient progress is not a sign of failure; it is often evidence that you are building something with depth, commitment, and sustainability.

Patience becomes one of the most important disciplines on the path to achievement. Strategic progress requires thoughtful decisions, consistent effort, and the willingness to trust the process even when results are not immediately visible. Every step forward, no matter how small, contributes to the realization of your vision. When you embrace patient progress, you shift your focus from rushing toward outcomes to faithfully executing the work required to achieve them.

MOMENT OF REFLECTION

Where in your life might impatience be causing you to overlook the progress you are already making toward your long term vision?

INTENTIONAL APPLICATION

Take a moment today to reflect on how far you have already come toward your goal and vision for your life. Write down three milestones, lessons, or improvements you made toward your goal and vision.

Take a moment to recognize your progress and remind yourself that success is built through steady, intentional action over time.

PERSONAL INSIGHTS

Confidence and Mindset

Day 21

Empower yourself by saying, I can do hard things.

DAILY INSIGHT

Life inevitably presents moments that test our resilience, courage, and perseverance. When faced with difficulty, our first instinct may be to doubt our ability to overcome the challenge. Yet the words we speak to ourselves have tremendous power. Affirming "I can do hard things" is more than a motivational phrase. It is a declaration of strength. It reminds us that growth often occurs outside of our comfort zone and that the challenges we face are opportunities to develop greater confidence and capability.

Believing in your ability to endure and overcome difficulty builds discipline and resilience. Each time you face something hard and continue forward, you reinforce the truth that you are capable of more than you can even grasp or realize. Hard moments shape character, deepen determination, and expand the limits of what we think is possible. By empowering yourself with a can-do mindset, you transform obstacles from barriers into stepping stones on your path toward growth.

MOMENT OF REFLECTION

What challenge in your life right now feels difficult but could become an opportunity to strengthen your confidence and resilience if you chose to face it with courage?

INTENTIONAL APPLICATION

Identify one task, conversation, or responsibility you have been avoiding because it feels daunting. Write down the statement "I can do hard things" and place it somewhere visible. Then commit to taking the first step toward that challenge today, reminding yourself that strength grows each time you choose courage over avoidance.

PERSONAL INSIGHTS

Day 22

Happiness is rooted in hope and the belief that things will get better.

DAILY INSIGHT

Happiness depends on what is happening and it is often misunderstood as a constant state of perfect circumstances. In reality, happiness is deeply connected to perspective and belief. Even during arduous seasons, hope has the power to sustain our sense of peace and optimism. When we believe that improvement is possible and that tomorrow can bring new opportunities, healing, and clarity, we cultivate a mindset that allows happiness to exist even in the midst of uncertainty. Hope becomes the quiet assurance that challenges are temporary and that growth and better days are ahead.

This belief requires discipline because life will inevitably present moments that test our optimism. Choosing hope is an intentional act of resilience. It means refusing to let temporary setbacks define your outlook on life. When you nurture hope, you strengthen your ability to endure adversity and remain open to the possibilities that the future holds. Over time, this hopeful mindset becomes a foundation for meaningful growth.

MOMENT OF REFLECTION

When life is life-ing, what helps you maintain hope and the belief that better days are still ahead?

INTENTIONAL APPLICATION

Write down three things in your life that give you hope for the future, whether they are relationships, personal goals, opportunities, or areas where you are growing. Take a moment to reflect on how these sources of hope can guide your mindset and remind you that progress and positive change are always possible.

PERSONAL INSIGHTS

Day 23

Mentality manifests your reality.

DAILY INSIGHT

You are what you think, and the way you think about your life has a powerful influence on the life you ultimately create. Your mentality, beliefs, expectations, and internal dialogue shape the way you interpret life's trials. Your thinking also affects your approach to opportunities and the way you respond to adversity. When your mindset is grounded in possibility, discipline, and resilience, you begin to act in ways that align with those beliefs. Over time, a positive mindset creates actions which influence the results you experience which, in turn, shapes your reality.

Life will not always unfold exactly as you hope, but it does mean that your mindset determines how you navigate what comes your way. A mentality focused on growth encourages persistence, creativity, and faith in your ability to improve your life. When you intentionally cultivate a mindset that believes in progress and purpose, you position yourself to recognize opportunities, overcome setbacks, and create a life that reflects your highest potential.

MOMENT OF REFLECTION

What beliefs or mental habits might currently be shaping the reality you are experiencing in your life?

INTENTIONAL APPLICATION

Write down one empowering belief about yourself or your future, such as, "I am capable of creating positive change in my life." Keep that statement visible throughout the day and intentionally allow it to guide your thoughts, decisions, and actions.

By reinforcing a mindset rooted in possibility and confidence, you begin to shape a reality that reflects the beliefs you choose to carry.

PERSONAL INSIGHTS

Day 24

A powerful lesson is realizing that you do not need anyone's permission to thrive; you simply need to move forward with confident boldness.

DAILY INSIGHT

One of the most liberating realizations in life is understanding that your growth, purpose, and success do not require the approval of others. Too often, people wait for validation, recognition, or encouragement before pursuing what they truly desire. While support from others can be valuable, your ability to thrive ultimately depends on your willingness to believe in yourself and take action. Confident boldness is the mindset that allows you to step forward even when others may not fully understand your vision.

Thriving begins when you trust your instincts, honor your goals, and move forward with courage. Boldness does not mean acting without thought; it means choosing progress over hesitation and belief over doubt. When you stop seeking permission and start embracing responsibility for your path, you reclaim control over your life's direction. Each step taken with confidence reinforces the truth that your potential is not determined by external approval but by the determination and discipline you bring to your journey.

MOMENT OF REFLECTION

Is there a goal, idea, or dream you have been postponing because you are waiting for approval or validation from someone else?

INTENTIONAL APPLICATION

Identify one goal or idea that excites you and take a small step toward it with confidence. It could be writing down a plan, starting a business, or sharing your vision with someone who encourages your growth.

By choosing to act with confidence, you reinforce the belief that thriving begins the moment you trust yourself and move forward with bold intention.

PERSONAL INSIGHTS

Day 25

Peace of mind produces calmness and ease, which are the real luxuries of life.

DAILY INSIGHT

Never forget that the most expensive luxury item is something you cannot buy, as it is time. In a world that often measures success through material wealth, status, or constant achievement, it is easy to overlook one of the greatest forms of true prosperity, which is peace of mind. When your mind is calm and your spirit is at ease, you experience a level of freedom that no external possession can provide. Peace of mind allows you to move through life with clarity, patience, and emotional stability, even when circumstances are uncertain. It creates the inner space necessary to think clearly, make wise decisions, and maintain balance in your daily life.

Cultivating peace of mind requires intentional choices. It involves protecting your mental and emotional well-being, setting healthy boundaries, and focusing your energy on what truly matters. Discipline in your thoughts, habits, and relationships plays a significant role in maintaining this inner calm. When you prioritize peace over chaos, you begin to realize that the greatest luxury in life is not having more things; it is having the calmness and ease that come from a settled and centered mind.

MOMENT OF REFLECTION

What habits, environments, or relationships in your life currently support your peace of mind?

INTENTIONAL APPLICATION

Make one intentional choice that protects your peace. It could be setting a healthy boundary, letting go of something that drains your energy, or choosing to focus your attention on what brings you ease. Write down your choice.

Remind yourself that peace of mind is not something you stumble upon, but that it is something you actively choose to cultivate.

PERSONAL INSIGHTS

The Power of Community

Day 26

Never underestimate the power of proximity; the right community creates transformation and a powerful sense of calm.

DAILY INSIGHT

The people and environments that surround us have a profound influence on the direction of our lives. Proximity to a supportive and growth oriented community can shape our mindset, strengthen our discipline, and expand our sense of what is possible. When you place yourself among people who encourage progress, integrity, and purpose, their influence naturally begins to elevate your thinking and actions. Transformation often happens, not only through individual effort, but through the shared energy and wisdom of those who walk alongside you.

Community provides a powerful sense of calm and stability. Knowing that you are surrounded by people who support your journey, can bring clarity during uncertain moments and provide reassurance. Healthy community reminds us that we do not have to navigate life alone. It offers accountability, encouragement, and perspective, which helps us stay grounded while continuing to grow. When you intentionally choose proximity to people who inspire and uplift you, you create an environment where transformation becomes possible.

MOMENT OF REFLECTION

Who are the people in your life whose presence encourages your growth, strengthens your mindset, and brings a sense of calm to your journey?

INTENTIONAL APPLICATION

Make a plan to intentionally connect with someone who contributes positively to your growth or sense of community today. Send them a message of appreciation, schedule time to talk, or simply share a moment of encouragement with them. Write down what you would like your message of appreciation to communicate. Nurturing relationships that uplift and support you helps strengthen the environment where transformation and peace can flourish.

PERSONAL INSIGHTS

Day 27

In friendship and in life, being understood is more important than the number of years you have known someone.

DAILY INSIGHT

Many people assume that the strength of a relationship is measured by how long someone has been in their life. While shared history can be meaningful, the true depth of a relationship is often defined by something far more powerful, which is the ability to feel understood. Being understood means that someone sees you clearly, respects your perspective, and values your experiences without judgment. This type of connection creates trust, emotional safety, and a sense of belonging that time alone cannot produce.

In both friendship and life, meaningful relationships are built on authenticity and mutual understanding. When people genuinely listen, support your growth, and appreciate who you are becoming, then those connections strengthen your sense of purpose and well-being. Surrounding yourself with people who understand and uplift you, allows you to move through life with greater confidence and peace. It reminds you that the quality of your relationships matters far more than their duration.

MOMENT OF REFLECTION

Do the relationships in your life make you feel genuinely understood, supported, and valued for who you are?

INTENTIONAL APPLICATION

Identify and create space for a deeper connection with someone in your life. Instead of discussing surface level topics, ask a meaningful question about their perspective, experiences, or aspirations, then listen with genuine curiosity. When we seek to truly understand others, we help cultivate the same depth of understanding that strengthens our most meaningful relationships. Write down someone with whom you would like to form a deeper connection.

PERSONAL INSIGHTS

Day 28

Love is seeing a gap and choosing to fill it, because when you pour into your assigned people, they will pour back into you.

DAILY INSIGHT

Love is most powerful when it is expressed through action. It is easy to speak kind words or feel compassion, but the truest expressions of love often appear when we notice a need and choose to step forward to help meet it. Seeing a gap, whether it is through encouraging someone, offering support during a difficult time, or assistance in completing a task, reflects a selfless form of care. These moments of intentional service strengthen relationships and demonstrate that love is not only something we say, but something we do.

When you consistently pour into the lives of others with sincerity and generosity, you create a cycle of mutual encouragement and support. The people who experience your kindness and investment are often inspired to respond in the same way. Over time, these acts of service build stronger communities and deeper relationships. By choosing to serve where you see a need, you not only uplift others, but it also cultivates a network of connections and goodwill that enriches your own life.

MOMENT OF REFLECTION

When was the last time you noticed a need in someone's life and intentionally stepped forward to help meet it?

INTENTIONAL APPLICATION

I challenge you to pay attention to the people around you and look for one small opportunity to serve or support someone without being asked. It could be offering encouragement, lending assistance, or simply taking time to listen. Write down how you plan to help someone today.

Small acts of intentional kindness often create powerful ripples of connection and care.

PERSONAL INSIGHTS

Day 29

Like a bank account, friendship requires deposits to make withdrawals, and wisdom demonstrates which invitations deserve your presence.

DAILY INSIGHT

Relationships, like financial investments, require intentional contributions over time. Trust, support, encouragement, and genuine care are the deposits that strengthen meaningful friendships. When we consistently invest in the well-being of others, we build relationships that are resilient and supportive during both good seasons and challenging ones. Just as a bank account cannot sustain withdrawals without deposits, friendships flourish when we intentionally nurture them through presence, kindness, and reliability.

At the same time, wisdom calls for discernment about where we choose to invest our time and energy. Not every invitation, opportunity, or social connection will align with your values, goals, or well-being. Learning to thoughtfully evaluate where your presence is most meaningful helps protect your peace and ensures that your energy is directed toward relationships and environments that support your growth. When we balance generosity with discernment, we cultivate relationships that are both healthy and fulfilling.

MOMENT OF REFLECTION

Are you intentionally making deposits into the relationships that matter most while also being discerning about where you invest your time and presence?

INTENTIONAL APPLICATION

Reflect on the people and spaces that truly enrich your life. Make a conscious decision to deepen your investment in the relationships that uplift your spirit while honoring your wisdom about where your presence is most valuable. Write down which spaces bring value to your life.

True connection grows when we choose to invest our time, attention, and care where it can create the greatest impact.

PERSONAL INSIGHTS

DAY 30

Forgiveness frees you for your future.

DAILY INSIGHT

Holding on to resentment, anger, or past hurt can quietly weigh down our lives. While the experience that caused the pain in the past is real, the emotional burden of holding on to negativity can continue to influence our present if we allow it to remain unresolved. Forgiveness does not mean that what happened was acceptable, nor does it require forgetting the lesson learned. Instead, forgiveness is a conscious decision to release the emotional grip that toxicity has on your life so that it no longer controls your thoughts, your peace, or your direction.

When you choose forgiveness, you create space for healing, growth, and advancement. It is an act of strength that allows you to reclaim your emotional freedom and redirect your energy toward building the future you desire. By letting go of what once wounded you, you free yourself from being defined by the past and open the door to a life guided by clarity, peace, and renewed possibility.

MOMENT OF REFLECTION

Is there a past hurt or disappointment that may still be holding your attention and preventing you from fully embracing your future?

INTENTIONAL APPLICATION

Take a few quiet moments today to reflect on a situation or a person you may need to forgive; this can include forgiving yourself. Write down what you learned from that experience and remind yourself that releasing the burden of resentment is a step toward reclaiming your peace.

Forgiveness is not about the past, it is about freeing your heart and mind for the life that is ahead of you. You got this!

PERSONAL INSIGHTS

Change Management

DAY 31

You cannot change what you do not confront; discomfort is necessary for growth.

DAILY INSIGHT

Growth rarely happens in places of complete comfort. Many of the most meaningful changes in life begin the moment we are willing to honestly confront the areas that need improvement. Avoidance can feel easier in the moment, but it often delays the transformation we truly desire. When we face challenges, habits, or situations that require change, we create the opportunity for progress. Confronting what is difficult requires courage, but it also opens the door to personal development and greater self-awareness.

Discomfort is often a sign that growth is taking place.

Just as muscles strengthen through resistance, our character, discipline, and perspective are refined when we face situations that stretch us beyond our comfort zone. By embracing discomfort rather than resisting it, we learn valuable lessons about resilience and determination. Each time we confront what needs to change, we move one step closer to becoming the person we are capable of being.

MOMENT OF REFLECTION

What is one area of your life that you may have been avoiding confronting, even though you know addressing it could lead to meaningful growth?

INTENTIONAL APPLICATION

Choose one situation, habit, or challenge you have been avoiding and take a moment today to acknowledge it honestly. Write down one constructive step you can take today to begin addressing it, even if the step feels small.

Growth begins the moment you have the courage to face what once felt uncomfortable.

PERSONAL INSIGHTS

Day 32

Never underestimate the power of your tailwind; it is possible to start late and arrive early. Know that a delay does not interfere with your destiny.

DAILY INSIGHT

It is possible to start late and arrive early. Life does not always unfold according to the timeline we originally imagine. Sometimes opportunities appear later than expected, progress feels delayed, or the path forward seems slower than others around us. In those moments, it is easy to believe that we are behind or that we have missed our chance. Yet life often works in ways that are not immediately visible. There are times in life when a tailwind, which is unseen forces of preparation, growth, and alignment, come together to propel you forward at precisely the right moment. When this synergy happens, it allows you to move farther and faster than you once thought possible.

Delays are not always denials; many times they are seasons of preparation. The lessons you learn, the character you develop, and the experiences you gain during these periods strengthen your ability to handle the opportunities ahead. When the right moment arrives, the progress you once felt was slow can suddenly accelerate. Trusting that your journey unfolds with purpose, allows you to remain patient, disciplined, and hopeful, knowing that your destiny is not determined by how quickly you start, but by your commitment to continue moving forward.

MOMENT OF REFLECTION

Have you ever felt delayed in pursuing a goal or dream, only to later realize that the timing allowed you to grow into the person capable of achieving it?

INTENTIONAL APPLICATION

Remind yourself that your journey does not have to follow someone else's timeline. Write down one goal or dream that still matters to you and take a moment to reaffirm your commitment to it. By focusing on steady progress rather than comparison, you honor the path that is uniquely unfolding for you.

PERSONAL INSIGHTS

DAY 33

A hard but true lesson, sometimes growth actually hurts, but it is worth it.

DAILY INSIGHT

Change sometimes hurts, and while growth is often celebrated as something exciting and empowering, the truth is it can also be uncomfortable and painful at times. Real growth requires us to confront difficult truths, release habits that no longer serve us, and stretch beyond the limits of what feels familiar. These moments of discomfort can challenge our patience and resilience, yet they are often the very experiences that shape our character and deepen our understanding of ourselves.

Just as physical muscles grow stronger through resistance, personal growth is often strengthened through struggle and challenge. The discomfort we experience during periods of transformation is not a sign that something is wrong; however, it is often evidence that meaningful change is taking place. When we trust that the lessons learned through hardship are preparing us for greater strength and clarity, we begin to see that the temporary pain of growth can lead to a life that has lasting meaning and satisfaction.

MOMENT OF REFLECTION

What growth area or uncomfortable experience in your life may actually be shaping you into a stronger, wiser version of yourself?

INTENTIONAL APPLICATION

Take a moment to reframe one difficult experience you are currently facing. Instead of viewing it only as a hardship, ask yourself what strength, lesson, or perspective it might be developing within you. Write down a lesson this experience has taught you.

Recognizing the value hidden within discomfort can help transform moments of struggle into stepping stones toward meaningful growth.

PERSONAL INSIGHTS

Day 34

If you feel like your life is stalling, change your surroundings.

DAILY INSIGHT

There is power in simply shifting to another location. At times in life, progress can feel slow or even stagnant. When this happens, we often assume the problem lies within our abilities or motivation. However, the environments that we put ourselves in, our surroundings, routines, and the people we interact with, all have a powerful influence on our mindset and momentum. A stagnant environment can quietly reinforce complacency, while a fresh or more inspiring setting can reignite creativity, focus, and determination.

Changing your surroundings does not always require a dramatic life shift. Sometimes it means just adjusting your daily environment, seeking new perspectives, or placing yourself among people who challenge and encourage your growth. New surroundings introduce new energy and new possibilities, reminding you that forward movement is always within reach. By intentionally shaping your environment, you create conditions that support progress rather than stagnation.

MOMENT OF REFLECTION

Are there aspects of your current environment, including your routines, spaces, or influences, that may be limiting your motivation or creativity?

INTENTIONAL APPLICATION

Today, make one intentional change to your environment that supports your growth. This could be working in a new space, spending time around someone who inspires you, or adjusting your routine to create fresh energy in your day. Write down the change that you will make. Remember, sometimes a small shift in surroundings can create the momentum needed to move forward again.

PERSONAL INSIGHTS

Day 35

Life is full of possibilities but to reach our goals, we must demonstrate leadership and be willing to try a new approach.

DAILY INSIGHT

Life presents countless possibilities, yet possibilities alone do not create progress. Reaching meaningful goals requires leadership which we must first find within ourselves. Personal leadership means taking responsibility for our direction, evaluating what is working and what is not, and having the courage to adjust when necessary. Sometimes the path we initially choose may not lead exactly where we expected, but true growth occurs when we remain open to learning and adapting.

Being willing to try a new approach reflects both humility and determination. It acknowledges that progress often requires experimentation, creativity, and the courage to step beyond familiar routines. When we shift our perspective or methods, we often discover opportunities that were not visible before. By leading ourselves with intention and remaining open to new ways of thinking and acting, we expand the possibilities available to us and move closer to achieving the goals we truly value.

MOMENT OF REFLECTION

Is there a goal in your life where a new approach or perspective could help you move forward more effectively?

INTENTIONAL APPLICATION

Take a moment to re-examine one goal or challenge you are currently facing. Ask yourself whether there might be a different strategy, habit, or perspective that could bring new momentum. Choose one small adjustment you can make today and observe how a fresh approach may open new possibilities. Write down your new approach/adjustment.

PERSONAL INSIGHTS

Embracing Your Inner Leader and Life Outlook

DAY 36

Gratitude and happiness are choices you have to make daily.

DAILY INSIGHT

It is thought that happiness is an emotion that occurs only when life is going well. In reality, inner peace is what produces happiness. Gratitude allows us to recognize the good that already exists in our lives, even during challenging seasons. When we intentionally focus on what we appreciate, our relationships, opportunities, lessons, and moments of peace, then we begin to cultivate a mindset that naturally nurtures happiness. Gratitude shifts our attention from what is missing to what is meaningful.

Choosing gratitude and happiness each day requires awareness and discipline. Life will always present difficulties, responsibilities, and moments of uncertainty, but our response to those circumstances shapes our emotional well-being. When we choose gratitude, we train our minds to notice possibility, growth, and hope. Over time, this daily decision transforms our outlook and allows happiness to grow from within rather than depending solely on external circumstances.

MOMENT OF REFLECTION

What are three things in your life right now that you can genuinely feel grateful for, even if you feel that your life is not perfect?

INTENTIONAL APPLICATION

Start a daily gratitude practice today. Write down three specific things you are grateful for and put them in a place that is visible to you so that it keeps life in perspective for the remainder of the day.

By pairing gratitude with intentional expression, you reinforce happiness within yourself.

PERSONAL INSIGHTS

Day 37

Never let fear stop you from making progress; there is more power inside you than you realize.

DAILY INSIGHT

Fear is a natural part of life. It often appears when we are standing at the edge of something new, uncertain, or important. While fear can sometimes serve as a signal to be cautious, it can also become a barrier that prevents us from moving forward. Many opportunities are missed, not because people lack ability, but because fear convinces them to hesitate. Yet progress rarely requires the absence of fear; it simply requires the courage to take action despite it.

Within each person, lies far more strength, resilience, and capability than they may initially recognize. The moment you begin to challenge fear with action, you start to uncover that hidden power. Every step forward, no matter how small, reinforces the belief that you are capable of overcoming uncertainty and rising to meet challenges. Growth often begins the moment we realize that fear does not control us and that our own volition to move forward is our driving force.

MOMENT OF REFLECTION

What opportunity or goal in your life have you hesitated to pursue because of fear?

INTENTIONAL APPLICATION

Challenge yourself today to do one thing that fear has been quietly discouraging you from doing. It could be speaking up in a meeting, starting a project you have been delaying, reaching out to someone you admire, or taking the first concrete step toward a goal you care about. Write down what fear you will overcome today and commit to completing that action before the day ends.

When you confront fear with action, you begin to discover the strength that was waiting within you all along.

PERSONAL INSIGHTS

DAY 38

Never underestimate the power of projection; confidence will take you places that even talent cannot get you into.

DAILY INSIGHT

Talent and skill are valuable, but confidence often determines whether those abilities are ever recognized or given the opportunity to grow. Projection and the way you carry yourself, communicate your ideas, and present your capabilities play a powerful role in how others perceive you. When you believe in your abilities and project that belief through your words, posture, and actions, you create opportunities that might otherwise remain out of reach. Confidence signals readiness, leadership, and the willingness to step forward when others hesitate. Never forget the PIE analogy: Performance, Image, and Exposure.

This does not mean pretending to be perfect or having all the answers. True confidence comes from trusting your potential and being willing to learn as you grow. Many people underestimate how much their mindset and presence influence their path. By developing the courage to show up confidently, you open doors to new experiences, connections, and opportunities that allow your talents to flourish.

MOMENT OF REFLECTION

Are there situations in your life where a stronger sense of confidence could help you step into opportunities that align with your goals?

INTENTIONAL APPLICATION

Challenge yourself today to take one bold action that visibly demonstrates confidence. Introduce yourself to someone new, share an idea in a meeting, apply for an opportunity you may have been hesitant about, or volunteer to take the lead on a task. Approach that moment with intention; stand tall, speak clearly, and trust your preparation. Write down your bold action.

Each time you project confidence through decisive action, you expand the opportunities available to you and reinforce the belief that you belong in the rooms you enter.

PERSONAL INSIGHTS

Day 39

Skeptics will always exist; shine anyway, because exposure to new possibilities opens exponential doors.

DAILY INSIGHT

In every stage of life, there will be people who doubt your vision, question your path, or struggle to see what you see for yourself. Skepticism is a natural part of pursuing anything meaningful or new. However, allowing doubt, whether from others or from within, to dim your light can limit the opportunities. Making the decision to "shine anyway" is an act of inner leadership. It means trusting your purpose and continuing to move forward even when your path is not fully understood by those around you.

Exposure to new environments, ideas, and opportunities has the power to expand what you believe is possible. When you remain open to growth and place yourself in spaces where new perspectives exist, doors begin to appear that you may not have imagined before. Often, the courage to step beyond skepticism, whether it be external or internal, leads to exponential opportunities for growth, connection, and purpose. By continuing to shine with confidence and curiosity, you allow new possibilities to shape the direction of your journey.

MOMENT OF REFLECTION

Have you ever not pursued an opportunity because of skepticism from others or even from your own doubts?

INTENTIONAL APPLICATION

Identify one goal, idea, or opportunity that you may have hesitated to pursue because of skepticism from others. Take one clear and visible step toward it, write down your idea and begin the first stage of the project. Be sure to place yourself in a space where that opportunity can grow.

Let that action serve as a declaration that skepticism does not determine your path. Your willingness to move forward and shine anyway is what ultimately creates new possibilities.

PERSONAL INSIGHTS

Day 40

Embrace the power of being different, because genius emerges when you tap into your unique talents and create the extraordinary from within.

DAILY INSIGHT

Many people spend their entire life trying to fit into expectations created by others, believing that success comes from blending in or following a familiar path. Yet some of the most impactful achievements in history have come from individuals who embraced their differences and allowed their unique perspective to shape their work and purpose. Your individuality is not a weakness; instead, it is a source of strength that can unlock creativity, innovation, and meaningful impact.

When you begin to recognize and develop your natural talents, you discover that the ability to create something extraordinary already exists within you. Genius is not always about extraordinary intelligence; it is often the courage to fully express the gifts, insights, and abilities that make you distinct. By embracing who you are and intentionally developing your strengths, you position yourself to contribute something valuable that no one else can replicate.

MOMENT OF REFLECTION

What unique talent, perspective, or skill within you could become a powerful source of impact if you chose to fully embrace and develop it?

INTENTIONAL APPLICATION

Identify one talent, passion, or creative ability that makes you uniquely you. Dedicate time to intentionally developing and expressing that gift, whether it is writing, creating, solving problems, helping others, or sharing an idea you believe in.

By choosing to nurture your unique abilities, you begin to unlock the extraordinary potential that already exists within you.

PERSONAL INSIGHTS

Closing Reflection

Congratulations! By reaching this moment, you have completed a 40 day journey of reflection, discipline, and self-discovery. That in itself is an accomplishment worth acknowledging. Over the past forty days, you made the intentional decision to pause, reflect, and invest in your personal growth. In a world that often moves quickly and demands constant attention, choosing to dedicate time to your own development is a powerful act of leadership.

Throughout this journey, you explored eight core themes designed to strengthen the foundation of a purposeful life: Identity and Purpose, Alignment and Self-Care, Resilience and Navigating Adversity, Focus and Execution, Confidence and Mindset, The Power of Community, Change Management, and Embracing Your Inner Leader while Developing a New Perspective. Each theme was meant to illuminate an important truth: growth is not accidental; it is intentional. By reflecting on these principles day by day, you have taken meaningful steps toward defining who you are and how you want to show up in the world.

The central goal of this journey was simple but powerful: to help you define yourself. Life often places expectations, labels, and narratives upon us, but true fulfillment comes when we decide to take ownership of our own identity and direction. Over these forty days, you have explored ideas that encourage you to think more deeply about your purpose, your mindset, and the choices that shape your life. The hope is that you now recognize that your story is not written by circumstance alone and that it is shaped by the decisions you make and the perspective you choose to carry.

One of the most meaningful shifts that can come from this journey is learning that you no longer have to be the last person on your own list. Your well-being, growth, and purpose deserve attention and care. When you invest in yourself, your mindset, your discipline, your relationships, and your vision, then you create a life that is more balanced, intentional, and fulfilling. Prioritizing your growth, does not take away from others; it strengthens your ability to show up fully in every area of your life.

As you move forward from this 40 day experience, remember that the journey does not end here. Growth is not a destination but a lifelong process. The insights you explored during these pages are tools, and ideally, these are tools you can continue to apply as new opportunities, challenges, and seasons appear in your life. The themes you have encountered can serve as guiding principles, reminding you to stay aligned with your purpose, maintain resilience through adversity, focus your energy on meaningful goals, and cultivate the mindset necessary to move forward with confidence.

There will still be moments when life feels uncertain, when obstacles arise, or when doubt tries to creep in. During those moments, remember the lessons you have embraced along the way. Remember that resilience is built through adversity, that focus creates progress, that confidence expands opportunity, and that your community can strengthen and support your journey. Most importantly, remember that leadership begins within you. The way you think, the way you act, and the way you choose to grow will shape the direction of your future.

Your next chapter is waiting to be written. Walk forward with the understanding that you now possess tools to navigate life with greater clarity, purpose, and intention. Continue to embrace growth, seek alignment, nurture meaningful relationships, and trust the unique gifts within you. When you embrace this inner power, you will not only create a life that reflects your values, you will inspire others to do the same.

Thank you for committing to this 40 day journey. May the lessons you have discovered here continue to guide you as you step confidently into the future you are creating.

The journey to define yourself continues. *You Got This!*

About the Author

DeGeorge Griffin is a proven problem solver, community leader, strategist, and a passionate advocate for personal growth and purpose driven living. A native of Southern California, DeGeorge spent more than seventeen years in the Washington, DC metropolitan area before returning to the West Coast. Throughout his career, he has built a reputation as a trusted problem solver and relationship builder, helping organizations navigate complex challenges and create meaningful outcomes.

Professionally, DeGeorge is an experienced senior business development executive with experience at companies such as Amazon Web Services, Thomson Reuters, and Gartner. Over the course of his career in the technology industry, he has worked with several billion-dollar enterprises, partnering with clients ranging from large global organizations to small business owners and entrepreneurs. His work centers on helping organizations leverage innovation, strategy, and technology to solve their most critical challenges and unlock new opportunities for growth.

Beyond his professional achievements, DeGeorge has always been deeply committed to service and community engagement. His passion for helping others led him to become a Certified Human Relations Facilitator through the National Conference for Community and Justice. This experience strengthened his dedication to building understanding, leadership, and connection among diverse communities.

DeGeorge remains actively involved in community initiatives and service. Over the years, he has served as a youth mentor, fundraiser, community organizer, nonprofit consultant, and as a Leader/Steward in the largest African Methodist Episcopal Church in the nation. His commitment to mentorship and leadership reflects his belief that empowering individuals and strengthening communities creates lasting impact.

DeGeorge earned his Bachelor of Arts in Communications from San Francisco State University and is a proud member of Alpha Phi Alpha Fraternity, Inc. Through his writing, leadership, and service, he continues to encourage others to embrace growth, define their purpose, and step confidently into the lives they are meant to live.

www.ingramcontent.com/pod-product-compliance
Lightning Source LLC
LaVergne TN
LVHW020716110826
845149LV00012B/2283

9781971868271